ANDREW *Johnson*

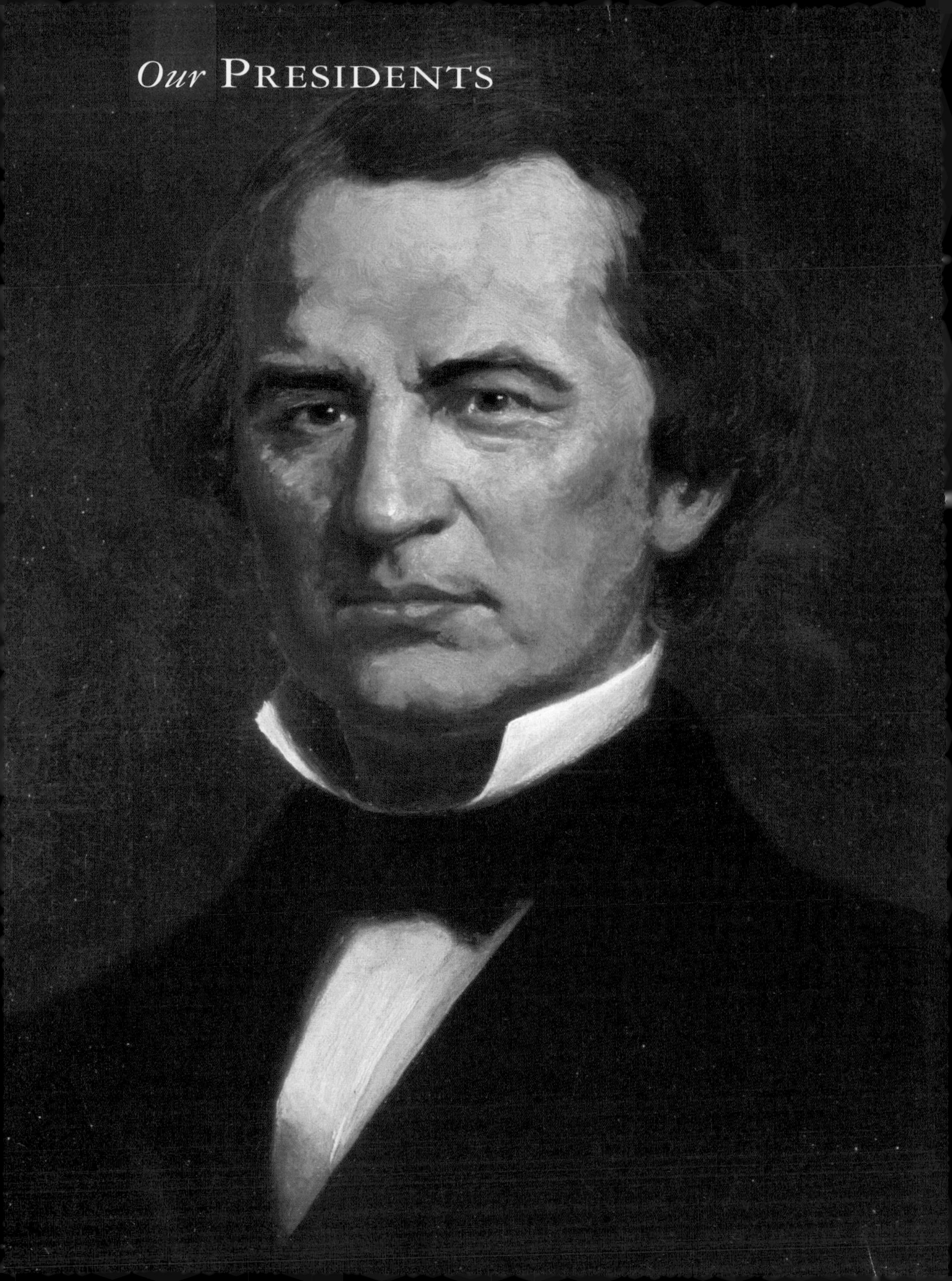
Our PRESIDENTS

ANDREW *Johnson*

Our Seventeenth President

By Judith E. Harper

SPIRIT
of America™

The Child's World®, Inc.
Chanhassen, Minnesota

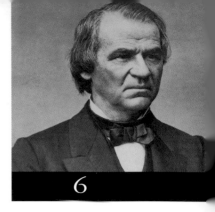

6

Andrew *Johnson*

Published in the United States of America by The Child's World®, Inc.
PO Box 326 • Chanhassen, MN 55317-0326 • 800-599-READ • www.childsworld.com

Acknowledgments

The Creative Spark: Mary Francis-DeMarois, Project Director; Elizabeth Sirimarco Budd, Series Editor; Robert Court, Design and Art Direction; Janine Graham, Page Layout; Jennifer Moyers, Production

The Child's World®, Inc.: Mary Berendes, Publishing Director; Red Line Editorial, Fact Research; Cindy Klingel, Curriculum Advisor; Robert Noyed, Historical Advisor

Photos

Cover: White House Collection, courtesy White House Historical Association; ©Bettman/Corbis: 34, 35; Chicago Historical Society: 19 (P&S-1920.1645; Artist: Paul Phillipateaux); 23 (P&S-1971.0177; Artist: Alonzo Chappel); Corbis: 13; Courtesy of the American Antiquarian Society: 25; Courtesy of the Andrew Johnson National Historic Site, Greeneville, Tennessee: 6, 7, 10, 11, 14, 18, 21, 24, 32; ©Kevin Daley 1997, Courtesy of the Homestead National Monument of America: 15; Library of Congress: 20, 22, 29, 30, 31; The New York Public Library: 26, 27

Registration

The Child's World®, Inc., Spirit of America™, and their associated logos are the sole property and registered trademarks of The Child's World®, Inc.

Library of Congress Cataloging-in-Publication Data
Harper, Judith E., 1953–
    Andrew Johnson : our seventeenth president / by Judith E. Harper.
        p. cm.
    Includes bibliographical references (p.   ) and index.
    ISBN 1-56766-854-2 (library bound : alk. paper)
    1. Johnson, Andrew, 1808–1875—Juvenile literature. 2.Presidents—United States—
Biography—Juvenile literature. [1. Johnson, Andrew, 1808–1875. 2. Presidents.] I. Title.
    E667 .H37 2001
    973.81'092—dc21

                                                00-011491

Contents

Chapter ONE	Poverty and Ambition	6
Chapter TWO	On to Washington!	14
Chapter THREE	Reconstruction	22
Chapter FOUR	Impeachment!	30
	Time Line	36
	Glossary Terms	38
	Our Presidents	42
	Presidential Facts	46
	For Further Information	47
	Index	48

Poverty and Ambition

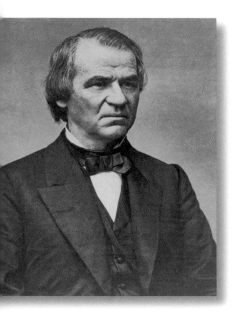

Andrew Johnson became the U.S. president in 1865 after President Lincoln died. Throughout Johnson's presidency, he battled with Congress to get things done his way. Finally, Congress voted to impeach him.

IN LATE 1860, THE UNITED STATES WAS moving rapidly toward a civil war between the northern and southern states. A civil war is fought between citizens from the same country. On December 20, South Carolina became the first Southern state to **secede** from the United States. Tennessee Senator Andrew Johnson, a Southerner, wanted the United States to remain one nation. He made a bold speech before his fellow senators. He pleaded with them to keep their states in the Union, another name for the United States. He was the only Southern senator to do so. This is what he said: "I [beg] every man throughout the nation who is a patriot ... to come forward ... and swear by our God ... that the **Constitution** shall be saved, and the Union **preserved.**"

In 1865, after the Civil War was over, Andrew Johnson became president. He vowed to reunite the country and to protect the Constitution. This was a difficult job in a nation that had been ripped apart by war. He tried to achieve this goal in his own way. He was convinced that his way was right, even when Congress and his advisors told him he was wrong. When Congress tried to force Johnson to leave the presidency, he fought back. He remained president until the end of his term. This is the story of the first American president to be **impeached** by Congress.

Andrew Johnson was born in this cabin in Raleigh, North Carolina, in 1808.

7

On December 29, 1808, Andrew Johnson was born in a two-room log cabin in Raleigh, North Carolina. His parents were poor, hard-working people. His father, Jacob Johnson, worked at a bank, keeping the rooms clean. He also served as a city **constable.** Andrew's mother, Mary Johnson, worked as a seamstress and laundress.

Andrew was just three years old when his father died. The Johnsons faced hard times after that. Mary's earnings were not enough to keep them from hunger. She remarried in 1814, but her new husband was not a good provider. The family slipped deeper into poverty.

Andrew had a deep longing for learning but never attended school. There were no public schools available, and his family could not afford to pay for a private school. This did not stop Andrew. He learned to read while he and his older brother William were **apprentices** to a tailor named James Selby. Of course, Andrew also learned the sewing skills that a tailor needed to know.

When Andrew was 15 years old, he and William ran away. They did this even though they had promised to stay with Selby until they completed their apprenticeships. But the boys were in trouble for throwing pieces of wood at a neighbor's house, and they didn't want to be punished. So Andrew and William walked to South Carolina, where they found work as tailors. Andrew then spent several years moving from one village to the next. He was always sure to find a job because he was such a fine tailor.

In 1826, Andrew settled in the mountains of East Tennessee. He later went to live in the

This map shows the United States around the time that Andrew Johnson was born. Johnson was a Southerner. He was originally from North Carolina but moved to Tennessee in 1826. Although he worked in the nation's capital for many years, he always considered Tennessee his home.

Johnson was a successful tailor in this shop in Greeneville, Tennessee.

Interesting Facts

▸ An educated man often read aloud to the apprentices and workers in James Selby's tailor shop. Andrew Johnson's favorite book was filled with the speeches of famous American and English leaders. He treasured these speeches so much that the man gave the book to him.

village of Greeneville. There he met Eliza McCardle. Eliza was fatherless, too. She and her mother were quilt makers. Andrew and Eliza were attracted to each other immediately. Within a year, they were married. She was 16 years old, and he was 18.

Andrew Johnson soon opened his own successful tailor shop. He employed a number of tailors, and his business grew. As he earned money, he bought property, which increased his wealth.

Andrew and Eliza had a happy marriage. Between 1828 and 1852, Eliza gave birth to three sons and two daughters. Eliza helped Andrew improve his writing and arithmetic. She had been lucky enough to go to school. Andrew loved books and read whenever he had the time.

In 1829, Andrew Johnson was elected alderman in Greeneville. An alderman is a person who helps to make the laws of a city. He and the rest of the aldermen made the laws for the community. Johnson was reelected to serve in this position several times. Each victory inspired him to go further in **politics.** He wanted to hold other, more important positions. Between 1834 and 1843, he served two terms as mayor of Greeneville and was elected three times to the Tennessee **state legislature,** which met in Nashville, the state capital. He served in both parts of the state legislature, the assembly and the senate.

As a politician, Andrew Johnson's greatest cause was to help ordinary working people—

Johnson bought property with the money he earned in his tailor shop. His investments in real estate made him wealthy. In 1830, he was able to afford this beautiful home in Greeneville.

▸ When Andrew Johnson had his own tailor shop in Greeneville, he not only hired tailors to work for him, he also employed men to read to his workers. He paid the readers seven cents an hour.

▸ Mordecai Lincoln, a cousin of Abraham Lincoln, lived in Greeneville. Johnson and Lincoln enjoyed **debating** each other. They also served as aldermen together.

farmers, craftspeople, and laborers. The state legislature was full of rich and well-educated men. Johnson believed it was his duty to make laws that would help people who were not wealthy. When he spoke to crowds of working people in East Tennessee, he told them that they, not the rich, were the most important citizens in the United States. He said that the labor of working people made the United States a powerful nation.

ANDREW JOHNSON'S ELECTED OFFICES

Andrew Johnson won his first election in 1829 and then held many different elected positions.

1829–1834	Alderman in Greeneville
1834	Mayor of Greeneville
1835–1837	Representative to the Tennessee state legislature
1837	Mayor of Greeneville
1839–1841	Representative to the Tennessee state legislature
1841–1843	State senator
1843–1852	Member of the U.S. House of Representatives
1853–1857	Governor of Tennessee
1857–1862	U.S. senator
1862–1865	Military governor of Tennessee
1865	Vice president (for six weeks)
1865–1869	President of the United States
1875	U.S. senator (for less than six months)

FROM THE TIME HE WAS a tailor's apprentice, Andrew Johnson was fascinated by politics. He loved to hear the speeches of famous leaders read aloud. He wanted to become a great public speaker himself someday.

He was not alone in his passion for speechmaking. Public speaking fascinated millions of Americans in the 1800s. Listening to speeches, lectures, and sermons was as popular then as going to movies or sporting events is today.

When he was a tailor in Greeneville, Johnson had a friend with whom he often disagreed. They enjoyed debating with each other. Johnson studied and practiced his public speaking whenever he could. Soon he was spending his evenings walking four miles to and from Tusculum College so that he could participate in debates that were held there.

As a young politician in Tennessee, Johnson became known as a great speaker. He had a powerful, clear voice. He was a fighter, and his opponents knew it. With his words, he "cut and slashed right and left … running his opponents through and through with a rusty jagged weapon." The crowds loved his toughness. His public speaking proved that Johnson was strong, intelligent, knowledgeable, and quick-thinking—exactly the qualities people wanted in a leader.

Chapter TWO

On to Washington!

Andrew Johnson was a member of the U.S. House of Representatives for 10 years, beginning in 1843.

AS ONE OF THE MOST POPULAR POLITICIANS in East Tennessee, Andrew Johnson decided to campaign for a much higher office—a seat in the U.S. House of Representatives in Washington, D.C. In 1843, he was elected.

In the House, Johnson began a long battle to help working people buy land. His own experience taught him how difficult it was for poor people to lift themselves out of poverty. He knew that land ownership helped him become successful. He believed that the government should make laws to help working people improve their lives.

Johnson worked hard to write and pass a law that would allow the head of every family to own 160 acres of government land. This **bill** was called the **Homestead** Act. Johnson

struggled to make it a law while he served in the House of Representatives and later when he was in the U.S. Senate.

In 1853, after 10 years in the House, Johnson lost his reelection campaign. He returned to Tennessee. There his defeat was soon followed by another victory. He was elected governor of Tennessee that same year. As governor, Johnson made changes that

In 1867, a man named George Washington Palmer built this cabin on his homestead near Beatrice, Nebraska. The Homestead Act of 1862 gave settlers 160 acres of land. Homesteaders owned their land after farming and living on it for five years.

15

helped poor people get an education. He convinced state lawmakers to increase taxes to pay for public schools and libraries.

In 1857, the Tennessee legislature chose Johnson to be a U.S. senator. Back in Washington, he continued working on his homestead bill. In July of 1860, Congress finally approved it. To Johnson's deep disappointment, it did not become a law because President James Buchanan decided to **veto** it. The Senate then voted on the bill again. It could still become a law if two-thirds or more of the senators voted for it, but they did not. Johnson's years of effort were not wasted, however. In 1862, when he was no longer at work on the bill, a new version of the homestead act became law.

Like his fellow Southerners, Senator Johnson supported slavery. He also believed that the Constitution gave the state governments the right to govern themselves. This included the right to decide whether an individual state would allow slavery. But, as he said many times, he did not believe that states had the right to secede from the Union. This was **treason,** he declared.

16

In 1861, one Southern state after another seceded from the Union. Johnson rushed home to Tennessee. He was determined to keep his home state in the Union. He gave speeches all over the state. Tempers were running high. People in support of the **Confederacy** were angry with **Unionists** like Johnson. A few threatened to **assassinate** him. The threats did not stop him. When Johnson spoke to crowds, he kept a gun with him so

In 1861, most slave states seceded from the Union to form the Confederate States of America. But four slave states decided to fight with the Union. These were called the border states because they sat on the border between the North and the South. President Lincoln and other leaders did not outlaw slavery in these states because the Union needed their support.

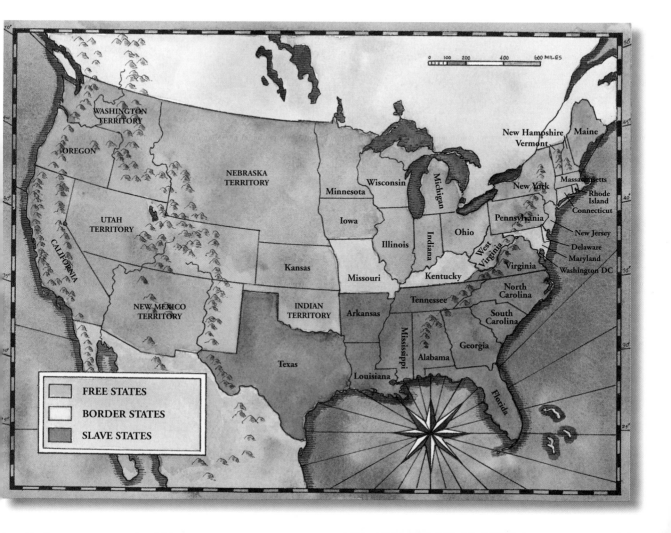

FREE STATES

BORDER STATES

SLAVE STATES

Johnson's wife Eliza suffered when the Confederates invaded Greeneville. They hated her because she was the wife of the most famous Southern "traitor." Unfortunately, she had tuberculosis, a disease that affects the lungs. She was too sick to travel to safety. For a long time, she had to stay in Confederate territory without her husband. Finally, she was able to join him in Nashville, which the Unionists controlled.

that he could defend himself if his life were in danger. Many people from East Tennessee wanted to stay in the Union. Unfortunately, the rest of the state did not. Tennessee seceded on June 8, 1861. With his battle for Tennessee lost, Johnson headed for safety in Kentucky, a slave state that had sided with the Union. He then traveled to Washington, where he was given a hero's welcome. He was the only Southern senator who served in the Senate after his state had seceded.

President Abraham Lincoln liked Johnson's courage, his toughness, and his devotion to the Union. He also admired Johnson's ability to stand up for what he believed. For all of these reasons, Lincoln appointed Johnson the military governor of Tennessee in 1862. Then Lincoln selected Johnson as the **candidate** for vice president in the 1864 presidential election. The two men belonged to different

18

The Union army, led by General Ulysses S. Grant, invaded western Tennessee in 1862. After Union soldiers defeated the Confederates at Fort Donelson, the Union took control of western Tennessee and Nashville. Then President Lincoln appointed Andrew Johnson the Union's military governor of Tennessee.

Although Abraham Lincoln and Andrew Johnson were from different political parties, they shared one important goal. They both wanted to save the Union.

political parties. Abraham Lincoln was a **Republican,** and Johnson was a **Democrat.** But they joined forces to run in the 1864 presidential election. Their new political party was called the National Union Party. It united all Republicans and Democrats who were Unionists.

Lincoln and Johnson won the election. On March 4, 1865, Andrew Johnson became the vice president of the United States. He served in this role for only six weeks.

20

WHEN THE UNION ARMY INVADED PART OF A CONFEDERATE STATE DURING the Civil War, President Lincoln appointed a military governor to take control. Andrew Johnson was the first to be chosen. In 1862, Lincoln made him a brigadier general and sent him to Nashville, Tennessee.

Johnson had a tough job. There was no state legislature to make the laws. He had to take charge of the government by himself. Most of the people in Nashville were loyal to the Confederacy. They hated all Unionists —and especially Johnson. He insisted that Confederates pledge their loyalty to the Union.

To make his job even harder, Nashville was in great danger from Confederate raiders. They attacked Unionists, exploded bridges, chopped up railroad ties, and blasted railroad tunnels. Despite the danger, Johnson stood his ground and held on to Nashville.

Many Tennessee leaders told Johnson that he was too hard on the Southern people. They said that his harsh rules made people hate the Union more. How would the people of Tennessee work together to rebuild their state after the war if there was so much hate?

Johnson did not listen to their advice. He refused to consider any **compromise.** He was sure that he was right to punish the Confederate traitors. After the war, it was very difficult for the people of Tennessee to work together.

Chapter THREE

Reconstruction

Andrew Johnson worked very hard as president, but his stubbornness often got in the way. He was so certain that he was right, he often refused to listen to advice or to others' opinions. He did not like to compromise with Congress. These qualities made it difficult for him to be a successful president.

IN APRIL OF 1865, THE CONFEDERACY **surrendered.** The American Civil War was finally over. Northerners were filled with joy, but Southerners were devastated. The war destroyed their land, homes, businesses, and farms. How would they survive?

The United States government faced an enormous challenge. How should it handle the Southerners and their problems now that the war was over? Before the government could deal with this question, a terrible tragedy struck the nation. On April 14, 1865—just five days after the South surrendered—President Lincoln was assassinated.

A few hours after Lincoln died on April 15, Andrew Johnson took the oath of office. He was the president of the United States.

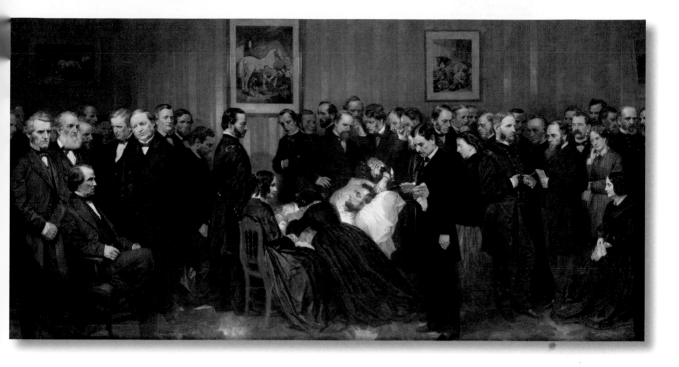

At first, Johnson vowed to punish the South for the war. But a few weeks later, he changed his mind. He realized that rebuilding the South could reunite the country. It also could make the United States stronger than ever. To achieve these goals, he knew that the South needed help, not punishment. Hurting the South would only weaken the nation.

There was another reason that Johnson changed his mind. Even though the next presidential election was more than three years away, he was already planning for it. He would need Southern votes to be reelected president in 1868. He thought that if he helped the South, the Southerners would vote for him.

Johnson is shown seated at left in this painting of Lincoln's death. Actually, Johnson was not present at the time. Because Lincoln's wife Mary hated Johnson, he was asked to leave the room a few hours before the president died.

23

Johnson **pardoned** many Southerners who had helped the Confederacy. In return, they pledged their loyalty to the United States. Johnson's **reconstruction** plan helped the Southern states govern themselves again.

When Congress met in December of 1865, Johnson's reconstruction plan had been at work for months. The majority of Republicans in Congress—many of whom were from the North—did not like Johnson's plan. They believed that the South was to blame for the war and should suffer for it. They were also worried about the fate of the newly freed slaves. Wealthy Southerners had enslaved African Americans for centuries. Could they be trusted to guard the rights of the **freedpeople?** The Republicans did not think so.

After the war, much of the South was in ruins. Men, women, and children in every Southern state were starving. Not only was there little food to eat, but there was no money, no livestock, and no seed to plant new crops. Many homes and other buildings were destroyed.

The Republicans had
good reason to be concerned.
By late 1865, the leaders of
the Southern states were determined that white Southerners
should have all the power.
They wanted African
Americans to be powerless. To
achieve this goal, the Southern
states, cities, and towns passed
laws called the Black Codes.
These laws limited the freedoms of African
Americans. They determined things such as
what kind of jobs African Americans could
have and where they could live.

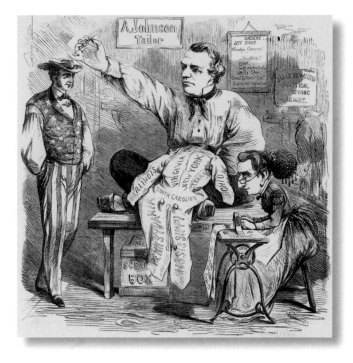

*This political cartoon shows
Andrew Johnson as the
tailor from Tennessee. He is
sewing the Southern states
and the Northern states
together to repair Uncle
Sam's coat. Unfortunately,
Johnson's plans to reunite
the Union failed. Congress
did not like his plans
for reconstruction.*

In 1866, Congress passed two laws to
protect African Americans in the South.
One arranged for some of the freedpeople to
continue receiving food, education, and land.
The other law was the Civil Rights Act of
1866. It declared that the ex-slaves were
citizens of the United States and had all the
rights of citizens.

President Johnson startled Congress when
he vetoed both bills. He said the laws were
unconstitutional because they took away the

African Americans in the South celebrated when the Civil Rights Act of 1866 became a law. They hoped this event would change their lives for the better.

rights of states to make their own laws. Republicans in Congress were angry about the vetoes. One group—the **Radical Republicans**—was especially upset. They never expected President Johnson to help the South and the ex-Confederates. After all, he had promised to punish the South! For the first time in U.S. history, Congress voted to **override** the president's veto. The Civil Rights Act became the law of the land.

The Radical Republicans realized the **Supreme Court** might decide that the Civil Rights Act was unconstitutional. So they prepared an **amendment** to the Constitution. Congress approved the new 14th Amendment, which guaranteed the right of citizenship of African Americans. It also kept ex-Confederates from being elected to political positions. As soon as three-quarters of the states voted to **ratify** it, the 14th Amendment would become law.

President Johnson believed the 14th Amendment was unconstitutional. He advised the Southern states not to ratify it. This made the Republicans even angrier. Johnson also believed that African Americans should be free, but he did not agree that they should have all the rights of white people. Like the majority of Americans in the 1860s, he had the mistaken belief that African Americans were not as capable or as smart as whites.

The Radical Republicans won many victories in the November elections of 1866. Now the Republicans were in control of Congress. They could override the president's veto much more easily and pass the laws they wanted. They would make sure that the ex-Confederate leaders did not rule the South. They would protect African Americans from unjust laws and violence.

The Republicans replaced Johnson's reconstruction plan with one of their own. The Reconstruction Act of 1867 carved up the Southern states into five military districts. A Northern general controlled each district. The generals made sure that each state wrote a new state constitution and formed a new government. Before a state could rejoin the United States, it had to allow African

The Ku Klux Klan (also called the KKK) was formed in Tennessee in 1866. The group then spread throughout the South. The KKK used violence—beatings, whippings, and murder—to control African Americans and white Republican leaders in the South.

Interesting Facts

▶ While Johnson was the president, his wife Eliza was very ill with tuberculosis. She rarely left her bedroom. Johnson's older daughter, Mary Johnson Patterson, carried out many of the duties of first lady. She redecorated the White House and acted as her father's hostess at parties and receptions.

▶ In 1887, Congress overturned the Tenure of Office Act.

American men to vote. It also had to ratify the 14th Amendment. Soon the 15th Amendment would enforce the right of black men throughout the country to vote. (Women of all races could not vote until 1920.)

The Republicans in Congress passed two other laws. These bills limited the president's powers. The Tenure of Office Act made it illegal for the president to fire the members of his **cabinet** and other government officials. He had to get the approval of the Senate first. The other law made it illegal for the president to send his military orders directly to the army. First he had to send them to General Ulysses S. Grant, a Republican. President Johnson was furious about these two laws. After all, the Constitution did not give Congress the right to take away the powers of the president.

For some time, President Johnson had been unhappy with Edwin Stanton, the secretary of war in his cabinet. President Johnson decided to fire him and test the Tenure of Office Act. The Republicans decided that this action was the last straw. They vowed to do everything in their power to remove him from office. The battle was on!

IN DECEMBER OF 1865, THE 13TH Amendment to the Constitution was ratified. It guaranteed that the nation's four million slaves were forever free. No one in the United States could enslave African Americans ever again. But were they really free? What were their lives like after freedom?

After the war, many black families in the South wanted to own small farms, but white landowners refused to sell them land. Many whites also would not rent land to African Americans or give them bank loans. As a result, African Americans had no choice but to work for white farmers who barely paid them enough to feed their families.

White Southerners passed laws known as the Black Codes. These laws varied from state to state, but they all had one thing in common. They prevented African Americans from living as fully free people. They also made sure that whites had all the power and that blacks remained poor and landless. In some states, African Americans were only allowed to work as farm laborers and servants for white people. The law closed all other jobs to them. The African Americans in this picture were laborers who picked cotton for the white plantation owner. They were paid very little for this back-breaking work, and their new lives seemed little better than slavery.

Some Southern states had laws that prevented black people from traveling from one village to the next. This made it difficult for blacks to hold more than one job. In some places, children were forced to work without pay.

In spite of all their troubles, African Americans kept their courage. They built strong communities and helped one another. They worshiped in their own churches and educated themselves and their children. And they waited for new laws that would allow them to be truly free.

Impeachment!

At the beginning of his trial, Johnson told his family, "They have impeached me for a violation of the Constitution and the laws.... Have I not been struggling, ever since I occupied this chair, to uphold the Constitution which they are trampling under foot?"

ON FEBRUARY 24, 1868, THE HOUSE OF Representatives voted to impeach President Andrew Johnson by a vote of 128 to 47. The House delivered 11 articles (reasons) for the impeachment. Most of the articles were connected to Johnson's firing of Secretary of War Edwin Stanton. Another article said that Johnson harmed Congress when he criticized it in his speeches.

According to the Constitution, Congress can impeach the president if he or she is guilty of "treason, **bribery,** or other high crimes and **misdemeanors.**" The articles of impeachment did not accuse Johnson of treason or bribery. So the House considered his misdeeds to be in the category of "high crimes and misdemeanors." This is a difficult

phrase to define because the Constitution does not explain what it means. Members of Congress must decide if a president's actions are serious enough to be considered "high crimes and misdemeanors."

Johnson was confident that he did not deserve to be impeached. He continued to work as if this cloud did not hang over him. He chose the best lawyers to defend him.

After the Senate gave its reasons for the impeachment, the president's lawyers stated their case. They argued that Johnson could not be found guilty of violating the Tenure

From February through May of 1868, the nation was buzzing with talk about the impeachment of President Johnson. Newspapers were full of articles, pictures, and stories about the trial. Crowds of men and women jammed the galleries of Congress, eager to witness the startling events.

31

of Office Act. They explained that the law was unconstitutional. Not only that, but President Abraham Lincoln had appointed Stanton, not Johnson. The law did not even apply in this case.

On May 16, the senators voted on one article. Thirty-five senators voted to convict Johnson, or find him guilty. All of them were Republicans. Another 19 voted to **acquit** him, including seven Republicans. The senators did not have enough votes to convict President Johnson—they were one vote short! On May 26, the senators voted on two more articles. The results were exactly the same. They were still one vote short. The Senate then voted to end the trial. President Johnson was acquitted! He could now finish his term. He also could campaign for his reelection.

Why did the impeachment trial fail to convict Johnson? There were many reasons, but one was very important. Some senators (even some Republicans) realized that if Johnson were convicted, any future president

Tickets were sold to citizens who wanted to attend the impeachment of President Johnson.

who disagreed with Congress might be forced out of office. This would harm the nation. The Constitution gives the president the right to disagree with Congress when he believes it is wrong. This is why the Constitution gives the president the power to veto the laws that Congress makes.

President Johnson was disappointed when the Democratic Party did not choose him as their candidate for president in 1868. He had less than a year left to be president. In spite of all his battles with Congress, he still achieved some important goals. He approved the plan to purchase Alaska from Russia, and he tried to make peace with Native Americans in the West. He also successfully removed the French government from Mexico. This was a big accomplishment since the United States had hoped for years to remove all European powers from the American continents. Johnson also continued to pardon Southerners. On December 25, 1868, he pardoned all the ex-Confederates.

Johnson bought a large farm outside of Greeneville, where he planned to live at the end of his term. When he returned to

Interesting Facts

▸ A terrifying event happened during Johnson's final days as president. An insane woman entered the White House, determined to assassinate Johnson. She was seized and taken away before she reached the president.

▸ Many Southerners celebrated when Johnson was acquitted. They fired off guns, had firework displays, and held parties.

Johnson did have some success during his term. In 1867, Secretary of State William Seward (second from left) purchased Alaska from Russia for about $7 million. Newspapers joked about it. They called it "Johnson's polar bear garden" and "Seward's Icebox." Americans later discovered how rich Alaska was in natural resources. Alaska was a huge bargain!

Tennessee in March 1869, he stayed active in politics. In 1874, he was elected U.S. senator. He returned to Washington, D.C., in 1875 but only served a few months. On a trip to Tennessee, he suffered a stroke. He died a few days later on July 31, 1875. He was 66 years old.

On March 20, 1875, Senator Johnson spoke to his fellow senators for the last time. His final words were, "May God bless this people, may God save the Constitution."

WHEN THE UNITED STATES WAS A NEW NATION, THE MEN WHO WROTE THE Constitution understood that someday a president might be involved in a crime. Or, that the president might do something so wrong that he (or she) should no longer be president. The Constitution gives Congress the power to: 1. impeach the president, 2. put him on trial, 3. convict him, and 4. remove him from office. This is how the impeachment process works:

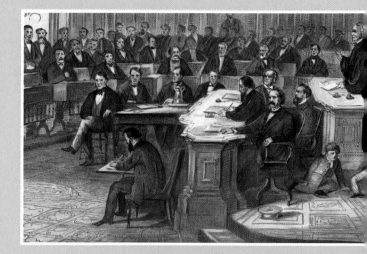

1. According to the Constitution, if a majority of members of the House of Representatives vote that they believe the president has committed "treason, bribery, or other high crimes and misde- meanors," then they have impeached the president. Two presidents have been impeached, Andrew Johnson in 1868 and William Clinton in 1998. In 1974, President Richard Nixon resigned before the House voted to impeach him.

2. Once the House has impeached the president, the Senate must put the president on trial. During the trial, the Senate presents evidence of the pres- ident's wrongdoing. The president's lawyers defend his actions. Then the senators vote. If two-thirds or more of the senators vote to convict him, then the president must be removed from office. If fewer than two-thirds of the senators vote to convict, then the president is acquitted and remains in office. (The Constitution also allows Congress to impeach the vice presi- dent and other "civil officers of the United States." Civil officers include judges and other important government officials.)

1808 Andrew Johnson is born in Raleigh, North Carolina on December 29.

1812 Jacob Johnson, Andrew Johnson's father, dies.

1822 At age 13, Johnson becomes an apprentice to James Selby, a tailor in Raleigh. He joins his older brother William, who is already an apprentice.

1824 The Johnson brothers leave their apprenticeships and run away from Raleigh.

1826 Johnson settles in East Tennessee.

1827 Johnson marries Eliza McCardle of Greeneville, Tennessee. Johnson sets up his own tailor shop.

1829 Johnson is elected alderman in Greeneville. He is reelected in 1830 and 1831.

1834 Johnson is elected mayor of Greeneville.

1835 Johnson is elected as a representative to the Tennessee state legislature. He travels to Nashville to serve his term.

1837 Johnson is not reelected to the state legislature. Once more, he is elected mayor of Greeneville.

1839 Johnson is reelected to the Tennessee state legislature.

1841 Johnson wins his campaign for state senator.

1843 Johnson is elected to the U.S. House of Representatives.

1845 After a bitter, difficult campaign, Johnson is reelected to the House.

1852 The House of Representatives accepts Johnson's homestead bill, but the Senate later votes against it. It does not become a law.

1853 Johnson loses his seat in the House but is elected governor of Tennessee.

1855 Johnson is reelected governor of Tennessee.

1857 Johnson is elected a U.S. senator. When he arrives in Washington, D.C., he again works on his homestead bill.

1860 The House and Senate pass Johnson's homestead bill, but President Buchanan vetoes it. Johnson wants to run for president but finally decides against it. In December, South Carolina is the first state to secede from the United States.

1861 In February and March, Johnson demands that the Southern states remain in the Union. On April 12, the Civil War begins. Johnson fails to convince the people of Tennessee to remain in the Union. Tennessee joins the Confederacy on June 8. Johnson returns to the U.S. Senate.

1862 In March, President Lincoln appoints Johnson the military governor of Tennessee. Johnson returns to Nashville.

1863 Johnson struggles to govern Tennessee because most of its citizens are Confederates.

1864 Lincoln selects Johnson to be the candidate for vice president. In November, President Lincoln and Johnson win the election.

1865 On March 4, Johnson is inaugurated vice president. General Robert E. Lee's Army of Northern Virginia surrenders on April 9. The Confederacy falls soon after. On April 14, Johnson visits Lincoln at the White House. They discuss plans for the reconstruction of the South. That night, Lincoln is shot at Ford's Theater. On April 15, Lincoln dies. Johnson is sworn in as the 17th president. Johnson carries out his own reconstruction plan in the South. He pardons many ex-Confederates. In December, the 13th Amendment becomes law. The Constitution now guarantees the freedom of all African Americans.

1866 Congress approves two bills to help African Americans in the South. Johnson vetoes both laws. Congress overrides both vetoes, and the bills become laws. In the fall, Johnson campaigns throughout the North for the Democrats. He criticizes the Republicans in his speeches and turns many Northerners against him. In November, the Republicans win more seats in Congress.

1867 Republicans are now in control of Congress. They toss out Johnson's reconstruction plan and enact one of their own. They prepare a 14th Amendment to protect the rights of African Americans. President Johnson approves the purchase of Alaska. He successfully removes the French government from Mexico, an important achievement for the United States.

1868 The House of Representatives impeaches Johnson. The Senate puts Johnson on trial. Johnson is acquitted. The 14th Amendment is ratified and becomes law. The Democratic Party does not choose Johnson as its candidate for president.

1869 In March, Johnson ends his term of office. He returns to Greeneville, Tennessee.

1875 Johnson returns to Washington to serve in the U.S. Senate. He becomes the only former president to serve in the Senate. He dies several months later of a stroke.

acquit (uh-KWIT)
When public officials acquit a person, they decide he or she is not guilty of a crime. The Senate had to acquit President Johnson because they did not have enough votes to convict him.

amendment (uh-MEND-ment)
An amendment is a change or addition to the Constitution or other documents. The 14th Amendment guaranteed the rights of African Americans.

apprentices (uh-PREN-tis-iz)
Apprentices are people who learn a skill under the teaching of an expert worker. As an apprentice, Johnson learned to be a tailor.

assassinate (uh-SASS-uh-nayt)
To assassinate means to murder someone, especially a well-known person. Some people threatened to assassinate Senator Johnson.

bill (BILL)
A bill is an idea for a new law that is presented to a group of lawmakers. Johnson proposed a bill that later became the Homestead Act.

bribery (BRY-bur-ee)
Bribery is when a person offers money or another reward to others, hoping to encourage them to do something in exchange. The Constitution states that bribery is a cause for impeachment.

cabinet (KAB-ih-net)
A cabinet is the group of people who advise a president. The Tenure of Office Act made it illegal for a president to fire members of his cabinet.

candidate (KAN-dih-det)
A candidate is a person running in an election. The Republican Party selected Johnson as the candidate for vice president in the election of 1864.

compromise (KOM-pruh-myz)
A compromise is a way to settle a disagreement in which both sides give up part of what they want. President Johnson refused to compromise on many issues.

Confederacy (kun-FED-ur-uh-see)
The Confederacy is another name for the Confederate States of America. The Confederacy included all the Southern states that seceded from the Union.

Glossary Terms

constable (KON-stuh-bul)
A constable is like a police officer. Andrew Johnson's father was a constable.

constitution (kon-stih-TOO-shun)
A constitution is the set of basic principles that govern a state, country, or society. Johnson promised to protect the U.S. Constitution.

debating (dih-BAY-ting)
Debating means taking part in a contest in which opponents argue for opposite sides of an issue. Johnson enjoyed debating.

Democrat (DEM-uh-krat)
A Democrat is a member of the Democratic Party, one of the two major political parties in the United States. Johnson, like many Southerners of his day, was a Democrat.

freedpeople (FREED-pee-pul)
The freedpeople were African Americans who had been slaves before slavery became illegal. The Radical Republicans passed laws to help the freedpeople in the South.

homestead (HOME-sted)
A homestead is a piece of land settled by a family. Johnson believed that a homestead would provide a poor man with a living and a way to gain wealth.

impeach (im-PEECH)
If the House of Representatives votes to impeach a president, it charges him or her with a crime or serious misdeed. The House decided to impeach Johnson because he violated a law, the Tenure of Office Act.

misdemeanors (mis-dee-MEE-nurz)
Misdemeanors are wrongful actions that are considered less serious than actual crimes. At Andrew Johnson's trial, his lawyers argued that his deeds were neither crimes nor misdemeanors.

override (OH-vur-ride)
When people override something, they cancel it or set it aside. In 1866, the Civil Rights Act became a law when the Senate decided to override the president's veto.

pardon (PAR-den)
When leaders pardon people, they excuse them for their crimes or misdeeds. Johnson pardoned thousands of Confederates after the Civil War.

**political parties
(puh-LIT-uh-kul PAR-teez)**
Political parties are groups of people who share similar ideas about how to run a government. Lincoln and Johnson were from different political parties, but they were both Unionists.

politics (PAWL-uh-tiks)
Politics refers to the actions and practices of the government. Johnson had a long career in politics.

preserve (pree-ZERV)
If people preserve something, they keep it from harm or change. Johnson and other Unionists wanted to preserve the Union.

**Radical Republicans
(RAD-ih-kul ree-PUB-lih-kenz)**
The Radical Republicans were a group of Northern Republicans that wanted a severe form of reconstruction in the South. The Radical Republicans were determined that the ex-Confederates should suffer and struggle before they rejoined the United States.

ratify (RAT-ih-fy)
If something is ratified, it is approved by a group of people. If three-quarters of the states ratify an amendment to the Constitution, it becomes law.

**reconstruction
(ree-kun-STRUK-shun)**
Reconstruction is the rebuilding of something. Johnson's reconstruction plan helped the Southern states govern themselves again after the Civil War.

Republican (ree-PUB-lih-ken)
A Republican is a member of the Republican Party, one of the two major political parties in the United States. In Johnson's time, many Republicans were against slavery.

secede (suh-SEED)
If a group secedes, it separates from a larger group. The southern states seceded from the Union to form their own country after Lincoln was elected in 1860.

**state legislature
(STAYT LEJ-uh-slay-chur)**
The state legislature is the part of state government that makes the laws. Johnson wanted to help working people when he served in the Tennessee state legislature.

**Supreme Court
(suh-PREEM KORT)**
The Supreme Court is the most powerful court in the United States. The Supreme Court decides if a law is unconstitutional.

surrender (suh-REN-dur)
Surrender means to give up or to admit defeat. When there was no hope of winning the Civil War, the South surrendered.

treason (TREE-zen)
Treason is a crime against the government of a nation. Andrew Johnson believed that Confederates were guilty of treason against the United States.

**unconstitutional
(un-kon-stih-TOO-shuh-nel)**
If a law is unconstitutional, it violates or goes against the laws and ideas in the Constitution. The Supreme Court decides if something is unconstitutional.

Unionists (YOON-yen-istz)
Unionists were people who supported the Union during the Civil War. Even though he was a Southerner, Andrew Johnson was a Unionist.

veto (VEE-toh)
A veto is the president's power to refuse to sign a bill into law. Andrew Johnson decided to veto bills that he believed were unconstitutional.

President	Birthplace	Life Span	Presidency	Political Party	First Lady
George Washington	Virginia	1732–1799	1789–1797	None	Martha Dandridge Custis Washington
John Adams	Massachusetts	1735–1826	1797–1801	Federalist	Abigail Smith Adams
Thomas Jefferson	Virginia	1743–1826	1801–1809	Democratic-Republican	widower
James Madison	Virginia	1751–1836	1809–1817	Democratic Republican	Dolley Payne Todd Madison
James Monroe	Virginia	1758–1831	1817–1825	Democratic Republican	Elizabeth Kortright Monroe
John Quincy Adams	Massachusetts	1767–1848	1825–1829	Democratic-Republican	Louisa Johnson Adams
Andrew Jackson	South Carolina	1767–1845	1829–1837	Democrat	widower
Martin Van Buren	New York	1782–1862	1837–1841	Democrat	widower
William H. Harrison	Virginia	1773–1841	1841	Whig	Anna Symmes Harrison
John Tyler	Virginia	1790–1862	1841–1845	Whig	Letitia Christian Tyler Julia Gardiner Tyler
James K. Polk	North Carolina	1795–1849	1845–1849	Democrat	Sarah Childress Polk

Our PRESIDENTS

President	Birthplace	Life Span	Presidency	Political Party	First Lady
Zachary Taylor	Virginia	1784–1850	1849–1850	Whig	Margaret Mackall Smith Taylor
Millard Fillmore	New York	1800–1874	1850–1853	Whig	Abigail Powers Fillmore
Franklin Pierce	New Hampshire	1804–1869	1853–1857	Democrat	Jane Means Appleton Pierce
James Buchanan	Pennsylvania	1791–1868	1857–1861	Democrat	never married
Abraham Lincoln	Kentucky	1809–1865	1861–1865	Republican	Mary Todd Lincoln
Andrew Johnson	North Carolina	1808–1875	1865–1869	Democrat	Eliza McCardle Johnson
Ulysses S. Grant	Ohio	1822–1885	1869–1877	Republican	Julia Dent Grant
Rutherford B. Hayes	Ohio	1822–1893	1877–1881	Republican	Lucy Webb Hayes
James A. Garfield	Ohio	1831–1881	1881	Republican	Lucretia Rudolph Garfield
Chester A. Arthur	Vermont	1829–1886	1881–1885	Republican	widower
Grover Cleveland	New Jersey	1837–1908	1885–1889	Democrat	Frances Folsom Cleveland

Our PRESIDENTS

President	Birthplace	Life Span	Presidency	Political Party	First Lady
Benjamin Harrison	Ohio	1833–1901	1889–1893	Republican	Caroline Scott Harrison
Grover Cleveland	New Jersey	1837–1908	1893–1897	Democrat	Frances Folsom Cleveland
William McKinley	Ohio	1843–1901	1897–1901	Republican	Ida Saxton McKinley
Theodore Roosevelt	New York	1858–1919	1901–1909	Republican	Edith Kermit Carow Roosevelt
William H. Taft	Ohio	1857–1930	1909–1913	Republican	Helen Herron Taft
Woodrow Wilson	Virginia	1856–1924	1913–1921	Democrat	Ellen L. Axson Wilson Edith Bolling Galt Wilson
Warren G. Harding	Ohio	1865–1923	1921–1923	Republican	Florence Kling De Wolfe Harding
Calvin Coolidge	Vermont	1872–1933	1923–1929	Republican	Grace Goodhue Coolidge
Herbert C. Hoover	Iowa	1874–1964	1929–1933	Republican	Lou Henry Hoover
Franklin D. Roosevelt	New York	1882–1945	1933–1945	Democrat	Anna Eleanor Roosevelt Roosevelt
Harry S. Truman	Missouri	1884–1972	1945–1953	Democrat	Elizabeth Wallace Truman

Our PRESIDENTS

President	Birthplace	Life Span	Presidency	Political Party	First Lady
Dwight D. Eisenhower	Texas	1890–1969	1953–1961	Republican	Mary "Mamie" Doud Eisenhower
John F. Kennedy	Massachusetts	1917–1963	1961–1963	Democrat	Jacqueline Bouvier Kennedy
Lyndon B. Johnson	Texas	1908–1973	1963–1969	Democrat	Claudia Alta Taylor Johnson
Richard M. Nixon	California	1913–1994	1969–1974	Republican	Thelma Catherine Ryan Nixon
Gerald Ford	Nebraska	1913–	1974–1977	Republican	Elizabeth "Betty" Bloomer Warren Ford
James Carter	Georgia	1924–	1977–1981	Democrat	Rosalynn Smith Carter
Ronald Reagan	Illinois	1911–	1981–1989	Republican	Nancy Davis Reagan
George Bush	Massachusetts	1924–	1989–1993	Republican	Barbara Pierce Bush
William Clinton	Arkansas	1946–	1993–2001	Democrat	Hillary Rodham Clinton
George W. Bush	Connecticut	1946–	2001–	Republican	Laura Welch Bush

Qualifications

To run for president, a candidate must
- be at least 35 years old
- be a citizen who was born in the United States
- have lived in the United States for 14 years

Term of Office

A president's term of office is four years. No president can stay in office for more than two terms.

Election Date

The presidential election takes place every four years on the first Tuesday of November.

Inauguration Date

Presidents are inaugurated on January 20.

Oath of Office

I do solemnly swear I will faithfully execute the office of the President of the United States and will to the best of my ability preserve, protect, and defend the Constitution of the United States.

Write a Letter to the President

One of the best things about being a U.S. citizen is that Americans get to participate in their government. They can speak out if they feel government leaders aren't doing their jobs. They can also praise leaders who are going the extra mile. Do you have something you'd like the president to do? Should the president worry more about the environment and encourage people to recycle? Should the government spend more money on our schools? You can write a letter to the president to say how you feel!

1600 Pennsylvania Avenue
Washington, D.C. 20500

You can even send an e-mail to: president@whitehouse.gov

For Further INFORMATION

Internet Sites

Find out more about Andrew Johnson's life and presidency:
http://www.kids.infoplease.com
Search "Andrew Johnson" and select "Encyclopedia"

Visit the President Andrew Johnson Museum and Library:
http://www.tusculum.edu/pages/ajmuseum/index.html

Visit the Andrew Johnson National Historic Site in Greeneville, Tennessee:
http://www.nps.gov/anjo/ajnhs.htm

Learn more about the impeachment of Andrew Johnson:
http://www.impeach-andrewjohnson.com
http://www.law.umkc.edu/faculty/projects/ftrials/impeach/impeachmt.htm

Find out more about the lives of African Americans during the Civil War and the Reconstruction era:
http://blackhistory.harpweek.com

Examine photographs of African Americans living in the South during Reconstruction:
http://digital.nypl.org/schomburg/images_aa19/
Choose Category "Reconstruction"

Books

Kent, Zachary. *Andrew Johnson: Seventeenth President of the United States.* Encyclopedia of Presidents Series. Chicago: Childrens Press, 1989.

Malone, Mary. *Andrew Johnson.* United States Presidents series. Springfield, NJ: Enslow Publishers, 1999.

Mettger, Zak. *Reconstruction: America after the Civil War.* Young Readers' History of the Civil War Series. New York: Dutton Children's Books, 1994.

Morin, Isobel V. *Impeaching the President.* Brookfield, CT: Millbrook Press, 1996.

Index

African Americans, 24-29, 37
Alaska, 33-34, 37
Atzerodt, George, 24

Black Codes, 25, 29
Booth, John Wilkes, 24
border states, 17
Buchanan, James, 16, 36

Civil Rights Act of 1866, 25-26
Civil War, 6, 20-21, 37
Clinton, William, 35
Confederate States of America, 17, 22, 37
Confederates, 21, 24, 26-27, 33, 37
Congress, 7, 16, 24-28, 30-33, 37

Democrats, 20, 33, 37

Emancipation Proclamation, 26

15th Amendment, 28
14th Amendment, 26, 37
France, 33, 37
freedpeople, 24

Grant, Ulysses S., 19, 28
Greeneville, Tennessee, 10, 20, 33-34

Homestead Act, 14-16, 36

impeachment process, 32-33, 35

Johnson, Andrew
    acquittal of, 32-33, 37
    apprenticeship of, 8, 36
    birth of, 8, 36
    death of, 34
    education of, 8, 10
    elected offices held by, 12
    as Greeneville alderman, 10-11, 36
    as Greeneville mayor, 36
    impeachment of, 7, 28, 30-32, 37
    marriage of, 10
    as military governor of Tennessee, 18-19, 21, 37
    opposition to 14th Amendment, 26-27
    presidency of, 7, 22, 27-32
    public speaking abilities, 13
    as state representative, 14-15, 36
    as supporter of working people, 11-12, 14
    tailoring business, 10, 12, 36
    as Tennessee governor, 15-16, 36
    as Tennessee state legislator, 11, 36
    as Unionist, 6, 17-18, 37
    as U.S. senator, 16, 34, 36-37
    veto of Civil Rights bill, 25-26
    as vice president, 18, 20, 37
Johnson, Eliza, 10, 18, 28, 36
Johnson, Jacob, 8, 36
Johnson, Mary, 8
Johnson, William, 8-9, 36

Kentucky, 18
Ku Klux Klan (KKK), 27

land ownership, 14-15
Lincoln, Abraham, 17-24, 26, 32, 37
Lincoln, Mary, 23
Lincoln, Mordecai, 12

McCardle, Eliza. *See* Johnson, Eliza
Mexico, 33, 37

National Union Party, 20, 37
Native Americans, 33
Nixon, Richard, 35

Palmer, George Washington, 15
Patterson, Mary Johnson, 28
presidential veto, overrides of, 26-27, 33

Radical Republicans, 26-27
Reconstruction, 22-24, 37
Reconstruction Act of 1867, 27
Republicans, 20, 24-26, 28-29, 32, 37

Selby, James, 8, 36
Seward, William, 34
slavery, 16-17, 24, 26, 29
Stanton, Edwin, 28-32

Tennessee, 16-19, 37
Tenure of Office Act, 28, 31-32
13th Amendment, 37

Unionists, 17, 20-21

voting rights, 27-28

working people, 11-12, 14-15